For You on New Year's Day

GEVORG EMIN

For You on New Year's Day

Translated by

Diana Der Hovanessian

Introduction by

Yevgeny Yevtushenko

International Poetry Series
Volume IX

Ohio University Press
Athens, Ohio   London

*The publication of this book was made possible by a grant from
Michael D. Cheteyan II, in memory of his father.*

DONABED GHAZAR CHETEYAN
of Palou
1910–1976

*In 1915, my father was among the children who survived the first
holocaust of the Twentieth Century at the hands of the Ottoman Turks.
He reached Syria in the "caravans" that crossed the desert, settled in
Aleppo, and dedicated his life to his adopted country. He was nomi-
nated a lifetime member of the Syrian Academy of Arts and Sciences
and was known by all the presidents as "The Ambassador of Peace."*

*He died in the United States, far from his ancestral homeland, but
with dreams of it still in his eyes and heart. That dream, his dream, as
well as the work of preserving the culture of that homeland on other
shores, has been passed to our generation.*

MDC II

Ohio University Press edition 1986.
First paperback edition 1986 by Ohio University Press.
Printed in the United States of America.

Library of Congress Cataloging-in-Publication Data

Ēmin, Gevorg, 1919–
  For you on New Year's Day.

  (International poetry series; v. 9)
  1. Ēmin, Gevorg, 1919–   —Translation, English.
I. Der Hovanessian, Diana. II. Title. III. Series.
PK8548.E5A24 1986   891'.99215   85-25888
ISBN 0-8214-0834-8
ISBN 0-8214-0835-6 (pbk.)

Grateful acknowledgment is made to the editors of the following
publications where many of these poems previously appeared:

Ararat Quarterly: "Small," "Ararat," "Insomnia," "Oh, No."

Anthology of Armenian Poetry, (Columbia University Press, 1978) edited
by Diana Der Hovanessian and Marzbed Margossian, "Cloud," "By
This Age," "All the Saints," "The Projector."

Christian Science Monitor: "Horses."

Granite: "Pity the Poor Butterfly," "Waiting," "What is It?"

Paris Review: "The Block," "We Never Discuss Trapping Monkeys."

Poetry Now: "Lorca's Prayer."

Yankee: "Growing a Tree," "In the Orchard."

Mundus Artium: "Why Has This Ache," and "Clever Lamb."

Frontispiece
Large *khatchkar*, now at Edchmiadzin, Armenia. Khatchkar: icon of the
cross. The true khatchkar appeared in Armenia between the IXth centuries,
after the liberation from Arab domination. These monuments are stone
slabs, sometimes huge, fixed on bases. Unlike most signs, that simply
inform, the iconic sign is in close relationship with the object symbolized.
The khatchkar-cross is not only a representation, a pretext of expression of
decorative talent, it is a true icon of the cross.

ACKNOWLEDGMENTS

Several years ago a friend, Tamar Hajian, sent me some poems by
Gevorg Emin with literal translations thoughtfully jotted in the margins
to save me dictionary time. I translated the poems about Ararat for my
classes (in Newton where I was the visiting poet in the schools) as
perfect examples of images. My students, who were junior and senior
high school teachers, took the poems to their students, and came back
with enthusiastic reports from Emin's first English audience.

More translations were done when I met the poet on his cultural
exchange visit to the States and when I went to Erevan in 1981 and
1983. A few others were done with Tatul Sonentz-Papazian, Ardashes
Emin, Sonia Ketchian, and Edmond Y. Azadian. (Emin also asked
Edmond Azadian to translate his biographical notes and the
introduction.) All the rest of the poems were read and checked by Dr.
Marzbed Margossian.

Diana Der Hovanessian

FOREWARD

The first book in the International Poetry Forum's Byblos Series was
Marco Antonio Montes de Oca's *The Heart of the Flute* translated by
Laura Villaseñor with an introduction by Octavio Paz. The second was
Arthur Lundkvist's *Agadir* translated and with an introduction by
William Jay Smith and Leif Sjoberg. Yannis Ritsos' *Subterranean Horses*
in a translation by Minas Savvas and with an introduction by Vassilis
Vassilikos was the third selection. The fourth and fifth were Bulgarian
selections published simultaneously: Lyubomir Levchev's *The
Mysterious Man* translated by Vladimir Phillipov, and Cornelia
Bozhilova's translation of Bozhidar Bozhilov's *American Pages*. *A Bird of
Paper* was the sixth selection. This book had the additional distinction of
being the result of close collaboration between the Nobel Laureate
Vicente Aleixandre and his friends and translators Willis Barnstone and
David Garrison. The seventh volume was *Transformations of the Lover*
by Adonis (Ali Ahmed Said), translated by myself. Frederick H.
Fornoff's translation of Laureano Albán's *The Endless Voyage* was the
eighth Byblos selection. This present volume is the ninth in the series
and remains in the same tradition of providing translations of some of
the most significant poets in the world for an audience that would not
otherwise be able to read them.

Samuel Hazo
President/Director
International Poetry Forum

AUTHOR'S PREFACE

These poems should be my true autobiography. A writer's authentic story is the story of his spirit and exists in his books. External facts are the same for every man: he is born, educated at this or that school, travels through happiness and grief, belief and disappointment, love and marriage. He has children. He dies. And these are the facts of my external biography to complement what you will find in my books.

My father was a teacher.[1] And I was born in Ashtarag in 1919. You will have trouble finding Ashtarag on a map. In fact, you may not even find my homeland Armenia. Although it is one of the oldest centers of civilization in the world, it has shrunk so much, especially in the 1915–1920 period, contracted like Balzac's *La Peau de Chagrin*, that it has almost disappeared from history and the face of the earth.

But Ashtarag has been in existence since the dawn of history with its ancient vineyards (Noah planted the first vine right after the flood) and its rich architectural treasures of dolmens, khatchkars (cross stones), cave carvings, vishabs (stone dragons), churches, bridges and fortresses which date from the Sixth to the Tenth centuries B.C. when the Urartuan kings reigned in the region. According to some learned men the name is derived from Ishtar, the Khaldi god. Others say it comes from the Armenian word for lofty, referring to its mountainous position.

On these mountain slopes generation after generation of villagers cultivated vineyards. And wherever there are grapes there is wine. And the villagers not only learned how to make stout wines, but found the secret of staying sober after drinking huge quantities. As they drank, and as they drink, their faces light up, they float, they are inspired. And as all good drinkers know, they fall in love easily. In love with songs, life, women. Ashtaragtsis have reputations not only as lovers, but as singers and poets.

The many famous writers who have come from this place include the Fifth Century historian Lazar of Pharb (Ghazar Parbetzi), Catholicos Nerses of Ashtarag, Sempat Shahaziz, novelist Berj Broshian, scholar Gregor Ghapantzian, and astronomer Norayr Sissakian.

i

Even among the semi-literate and literate elderly are many Homers today writing the history of Armenia in secret books of poetry.

My own poetry springs from this town and the deep valley of the Kassakh river, where since my earliest childhood I heard the running stream. Granted, that at the time I was not aware of rhythm or rhyme in its flow; nevertheless, all my poetry originated from its sounds.

I don't remember much of my first year of schooling there in Ashtarag, but I know that whatever good I have in my soul comes from the dusty streets where I have played, from the Kassakh valley, from the Chapels of Garmravor[2] and Marineh, and from the witty, colorful folklore and songs of that village.

In 1927 our family moved to Erevan where after high school I graduated form the Polytechnic Institute as a hydraulic engineer in 1940. Today if I write instead of build canals and power plants it is due to two things: the impact of meeting the poet Eghishe Charents,[3] and second, the touch of the ancient manuscripts at the Madenataran library where I worked as a student and could read and hold the magnificent old manuscripts from the Fifth through the Eighteenth centuries.

Although I was later trained in philology, it was more my education as an engineer that I am indebted to as a poet because I believe the exact sciences have endowed me with the discipline and sense of form and construction, plus an abhorrence of the superfluous and the hazy, no matter how elegant or elevated the sound. The poetry of the East, in my estimation, has been hurt, rather than helped by the ''elegant'' and ''sublime.''

My first book of poetry was published the same year I graduated from the university. I took book and diploma with me to the region of Vertenis where I was entrusted with the construction of a hydroelectric plant. During the war I was drafted into the army, fell in love, married.[4] I have lived and studied in Moscow, traveled throughout the Soviet Union and abroad. I have been in Korea, France, the United States, Cyprus, Greece, India, Syria and Eastern Europe. My voyages have convinced me that all people are essentially the same in their happiness and disappointments, needs, and desires. My travel has also confirmed my opinion of the great role of literature in man's destiny.

I have published more than fifteen[5] volumes of poetry and prose. I have three sons, Vahan, Gregor, and Ardashes. I belong to a very small nation with a very old history, and a very large heart.

Gevorg Emin

[1]Emin's family name is Muradian.
[2]Magnificent Seventh Century church of reddish stone.
[3]Charents (1897-1937) is called the father of modern Soviet Armenian poetry. He died in prison during Stalin's time.
[4]Emin's first wife, who died in Moscow, was the only child of the great lyric poet Vahan Derian (1895-1920). His second wife is Armenouhi Hamparian, the writer.
[5]According to the directory of Soviet Armenian Writers, Emin is the author of thirty volumes of poetry and twelve books of translations. He has also written two volumes of prose and two film scripts. His work has been translated into more than a dozen languages, and has won every top Soviet literary award.

INTRODUCTION

Poetry critics have always attacked logic and reason in poetry and based their criticism, ironically, on logic. Emotion is the queen they have crowned on poetry's throne, forgetting to place the king of reason and rationality beside her.

Traditionally, Sergei Yesenin is presented as a purely emotional poet. But the entire body of his work, free as it is of rhetoric and didacticism, is a philosophy of metaphors for the love of nature, humanity, homeland. It would be ludicrous to credit him with the "merit" of lacking logic.

Emotions that rise from perception reach logical conclusions; just as ideas emanating from deep sentiment turn into feeling.

True harmony in poetry comes from the blend of both. And I am reminded of this in reading Emin's poetry. (Of course, I read in Russian translation, and much may be lost because I am not proficient in Armenian.) However, I have been acquainted with Armenian literature from classical through modern times, and I have found Armenian poetry always preserving, as if a sacred vow were taken, the unity of idea and feeling.

That inclination is especially conspicuous in the work of Avedik Issahakian, who proved the strength of simplicity, Eghishe Charents with his tense dramaticism, and Barouyr Sevag whose starkly simple style penetrates like a confession. I find the entire body of Armenian literary tradition a testament to the unity of idea and emotion.

Contemporary Armenian poets, Hamo Sahian and Sylva Gaboudikian and others, follow this tradition. Brilliant Hovaness Shiraz stands out as an artist who does not care if his poetry is branded old-fashioned just because it is made from the pink tufa of emotion. And he defies the use of cold rationality as a cement for his blocks.

Gevorg Emin has an entirely opposite conception of the craft. He takes pride in revealing the rational armature of poetry and the details of its construction. Some of his poems remind us of transparent watches where the movements and direction of each gear and lever are visible. But it is a watch that keeps perfect time. Precision is one of the conditions of authentic art.

In his *Seven Songs about Armenia*, Emin successfully synthesizes the formal ode in simple journalistic language, charging ordinary facts with emotion. In this book Emin combines the poetic and prosaic, the refined and the grotesque. His scathing wit lashes the foolish, his kind austerity leads the lost, and his almost-pessimistic sarcasm and enjoyment of life's blessings seem to redeem life's brevity.

There are poets and painters who after portraying any aspect of life on paper or canvas avoid any discussion of their product, either out of fear or coquetry. I believe coquetry and fear are the same thing in art. The fear is a terror of being branded with rationalism.

Emin is different. He does not avoid coming to conclusions or making statements of principle, even in the most intimate poems. He is for completed ideas, favoring the full stop, the period, over the exclamation point.

Not that I am blaming any poet for being suggestive or inconclusive. On the other hand, I consider it a poet's right to be final in his statement when he has the individuality to do so. And Emin does:

> *There are no quicker words*
> *than yes or no*

Emin's "yes" has nothing in common with practical optimism, nor does his "no" convey the same pessimism favored by those who eat rocquefort cheese. It seems sometimes that Emin considers life's ironies more important than life itself:

> *Am I winning or losing?*
> *I really don't know . . .*
> *Has old age found me*
> *or am I finding myself?*
> *Should I bother to find out*
> *or smile a sad smile.*

Emin is so clever he can actually look down on cerebral wisdom as in "The Fanatic Literati":

Should anyone sketch us
they would draw
only a huge head,
nothing more. A head
we consider full, but
which is crammed with
self-delusions . . .

In another poem for those who survive at the expense of others he portrays a son who grew up "only as far as his father's pockets." And he never grew more, emotionally. The poem jabs at those without inner life and people who, under the pretext of being failures, get by in life. Emin's poem "He Who is on Dry Ground" is pulled in two directions. It blames those who take advantage of their failures, and yet defends those who are truly deprived. Emin's emotions in this case, as in others, have only one source, but multiple targets.

Many Soviet poets, following Andrei Voznesensky's foot-steps, have written poems about strip tease, all critical of the dance. When I first read Emin's poem on the subject, I thought he was starting the same path, stripping the female body, and enjoying the healthy male's instincts along the way. But Emin's sensuousness is not wrapped in a hypocritical moralism. As often happens in his work there is a surprise ending. And the poem ends with a natural sigh of regret.

Emin has many poems inspired by travel or based on universal themes. In the mosaic of these he never fails placing the authentic Armenian pebbles soaked in blood and tears.

He writes in a simple traditional way about the destiny of Armenia, a tradition derived from ancient folklore and legends. His reference to the vine is typical, the vine being the symbol of the Armenian people, which, the more it is crushed, the stronger it clings to the earth and the hardier its fruit.

Until today Emin cannot forget the rifle butts of Janissaries which knocked down Armenia's gates in 1919. And he suffers for the scattering of Armenians all over the world.

Narrow parochialism is alien to Emin's poetry. His heartbeat is as receptive to Mesrob Mashtots (who invented the Armenian alphabet) as to the juicy words of Robert Burns or the torrential rhythms of Walt Whitman. Also, despite his bitterness toward the Turkish atrocities, Emin has translated Nazim Hikmet's poetry. In the twentieth century one becomes a true national poet only through a universal approach. And he attains his universal approach through poems such as this:

> . . . I would also court martial
> the flower blooming at the Gestapo door
> and the dainty crescent moon
> illuminating the scimitar
> cutting Armenians down.
>
> Yes, and the canary that sang
> near the crematorium at Auschwitz.
> And the piece of paper that allowed
> lies printed on its face.
> And the thing, the unnamed thing that
> allows all the above to be repeated . . .

In other poems the poet faces death with a smile because he considers there's no such thing for people who have not lived indifferently.

Other times he is convinced there is nothing "New under the moon." That does not discourage him from wanting to abolish all the "Middle Ages" from all ages.

Emin's favorite punctuation is the question mark.

> . . . What force bent you over?
> Did you not evoke once,
> call out, and stress?
> But you got weary of it all,
> got wise, and turned like this.

Emin uses the question mark like a hoist, to elevate the problems of modern times. But he not only raises questions, he provides answers. The poet's task has been compared to many things, including the work of a general, the voyage of the seafarer. So why not compare it with the work of the cook? Pablo Neruda, who also liked to praise the banquet table, would have appreciated this metaphor:

> *To prepare a bozbash*
> *all you need is lamb*
> *meat and two onions*
> *thinly sliced . . .*
> *. . . Oh, I almost forgot*
> *the most soul stirring spice,*
> *the delicious and secret*
> *ingredient found only*
> *in one strand of gray*
> *hair fallen from your*
> *mother's head.*

Like that delicious Armenian stew, Emin's poetry is rich with the body and the flesh of the twentieth century, the pungent taste of the onion, the pepper of sarcasm, freshness of the greens, salt of wisdom and all with Armenia's graying hair.

OH, NO (FOR GEVORG EMIN)

> *No,*
> *there is not a single Russian*
> *brother who does not want*
> *to share the Armenian pain,*
> *who does not want to join*
> *an Armenian over carefree cognac*
> *and jokes from Radio Erevan.*
> *There is not one*
> *in whose heart and soul your luck,*
> *your harsh fate is not felt;*
> *not one*

who does not mourn your loss
the way he mourns his own.
For we too have suffered
the catastrophes life can dole
and sacrificed on the same battle-
fields so many victims
our brotherhood is sealed now
in blood.
And there is no telling,
no one can tell, which brother
is the elder.
All this is not due
to thieves nor evil hands,
but blood. We are blood brothers
now and Ararat can scold
and call me the same way it calls
an Armenian.

The day will come, I know,
when boundaries
are erased from this world
and only the rainbow divides
earth and sky,
when I can clasp Ararat
to my breast freely . . .
or else
(if rage were strength)
lift the mountain to my shoulders
and though crushed down
by its sacred weight
move it by myself here to you.

Yevgeny Yevtushenko
Translated by Edmond Y. Azadian with
Diana Der Hovanessian

Contents

For You on New Year's Day

You are real.
and because of that, perhaps,
I can walk under clouds and rain
and not forget the sun.

On the coldest days
I remember there is fire
somewhere after all.

In the heat of sweltering days
I realize
that snow shimmers intact
on the peak of Ararat.

You are real,
and because of that, I see
beyond our room to taste life
with two mouths, four eyes.

You are real. And because of you
I think the spring to come
can have no fall.

What is it
though made of stone,
softens men of stone?

What is it
though made of ice,
warms men of ice?

What is it that draws
men to Armenia
though it is not there?

What is twin peaked
but a symbol of unity?

What is
neither reachable
nor out of sight . . .
like a great love?

Ararat?
Ararat.

THE PROJECTOR

I was talking,
prattling on,
listing things,
like an index,
this and that,
random happenings.
I would still be mouthing if
I had not seen
suddenly the twin
projectors
of your eyes
beaming blackness.
Their night
covered the city,
the forest and
cities beyond
until the whole
world turned black.
I was silent then.
The only alternative
would have been
to scream.

We stand rooted,
unblinking
eye to eye,
my mountain and I.

Faith, they say,
moves mountains,
as Noah moved you
into sight.

I am filled with
the same fanatic flood.
And still we are planted
stones.

I curse my own immobility.
It is for nothing.
This is Ararat.
I am an Armenian,
and we are apart?
For how long?
Satan knows.
I am transient. I am mortal.
I shall pass.

And you, my mountain,
will you never
walk
toward me?

SMALL

Yes, we are small,
the smallest pebble
in a field of stones.

But have you felt the hurtle
of pebbles pitched
from a mountain top?

Small
as the smallest mountain stream,
stopping rapids, currents
unknown to wide
and lazy valley rivers.

Small,
like the bullet in the bore
of the rifle;
small as the acorn
waiting to sprout.

Small
as the pinch of salt
that seasons the table.

Small, yes
you have compressed us,

[5]

world, into a diamond.

Small,
you have dispersed us,
scattered us like stars.
We are everywhere
in your vision.

Small,
but our borders stretch
from Pyuragan telescopes
to the moon,
from Loussavan backwards
to Urartu.

Small as the grain
of marvelous uranium
which cannot be broken down,
put out, or consumed.

THE BLOCK

For two months
I have not written
a word.

My voice, a low
grumble, disturbs
our quarter

like the rumble
of the millstone
which, having nothing to grind,
grinds itself.

Horses,
how beautiful you are,
how natural,
standing in the meadow
eye to eye,
head to head against
each other's mane.
You do not pierce each other's
hearts. How much more intelligent
than this girl and I
tormenting ourselves
with the sharp edges of words,
separations and subtle jousts
to crack the heart of each.
Oh I envy you, horses.

You know how it's done of course
with bottles and sugar. The monkey thrusts
in a paw and can't extricate
his fist without giving up his bait
and won't. He's captured thus.
But why should monkeys concern us?

Pity the poor butterfly
born to live just one day
and that one day it rains.

Pity the pilgrim home from his exile.
One week in Armenia
and that week it rains.

Ararat is clouded.
Sevan is misted.

Happy the man
who does not pity these things.

Something is going to happen.
I know it.
Each time I start to write I feel
the sharp foreboding of
something leaning forward:
the same feeling that comes before love,
when a glance or a touch on the arm
fills me with the pungence of a strange flower
or a new ointment
(or do I pour the fragrance into these?)

My nostrils flare
like the panther's
breathing in the shiver
of the unseen gazelle. But
I am bodiless. A fever.
A passion. A focus. A notch in time.
I wait for the silent deer, that drinking gazelle.
In whose eye will I drown? I do not know.

I only know I dread that perhaps
instead of love, a mocking flirtation;
instead of song, mocking sounds;
instead of deer, a rabbit
will spring upon me
ending my eagerness.

As if he never crawled,
as if he did not bite,
he lies here in state,
even dignified,

exactly like the snake
or like the worm
who never could go straight
until the day it died.

Who is to blame for this murder?
Who was it who placed
white Ararat,
spotless Ararat
in a pool of blood
to bleed
for centuries?

Whose idea
to make hell
out of Eden
in the shadow of Ararat?
Who gave us
instead of land,
an eroded road;
instead of earth, stones;
instead of springs of
water, blood.

Who?
And from the first dawning
of our story, who shoved the head
of this creative people under
the bloody sword of the invading
neighbor?

Who demanded his soul,
in exchange for his body?

Lord, give me, as you gave Moses
the power to uproot and remove
my persecuted tribe,
my indestructible tribe
with its new seed,
its ancient roots,
its old story and monuments
from this place
this land of death,
this pile of rock,
to another shore that is safe.
(But is there such a place?)

Give me, the word-worker,
the wand to split rocks
so they will gush water, give
me the staff to divide the red sea
of fortune,
dividing tears from blood, even
if, like Moses,
I find death and am buried
in foreign soil before
reaching the promised place,
even if I reach the beloved's door
to find it locked . . .

Oh Lord, are you deaf
to the red news of massacre?*

*Refers to a famous series of poems by Siamanto about the 1895 and 1904
Turkish massacres. Siamanto died in the 1915 massacre.

[14]

YES OR NO

There are no quicker words to use
as easy as yes or no
and yet some people live and die
before deciding which to choose.

A cloud is passing
through my heart
leaving a cold shapeless longing.
     And you, what are you doing
     right this minute?
     This cold, foggy night?
     Are you at home?
     With your face against
     the window glass
     watching for me?
Or are you out tonight
head high and laughing?
Well, you cannot escape
completely. I know
wherever you are
this cloud will pass
through your heart too.

Why has this ache returned,
the pain that's more
than one man's share?

There's no love left
but still it hurts
as if still there.

What is this punishment
that banished-love leaves,
as unfair as revenge?

I wake up in the night
as the amputated soldier does
with pain in that arm
he no longer has.

I imagined I had picked a peach,
but the design
to have me reach and pluck it down
was not mine.

It willed my teeth into its flesh
down to its slippery stone.
Then it wished itself flung in the yard
where it was thrown.

That peach picked me.

Sleep rejects me
on this rainy night.
The storm wears out the roof,
outflows the bucket in the yard,
pours into my skull
the sound of rundown houses
and their sorrows.
Sleep rejects me.

This spring's rain is poisonous,
breeds death.
Not only Hiroshima
blooms with
mutated forms;
my sidewalk and my yard
creep and crack
with strange growth.
Sleep rejects me.

It mocks my open eyes,
sticks to my lashes,
repelled by what it sees
inside. My eyes reflect
the speed of rocketships
to the moon and Mars.
And who knows how many
others also stare,
heart-burst, tongue-swollen,
eyes-propped open with pain,

stare back at my own blank eyes
this black night.

Man, what are you doing,
where are you flying,
faster and faster
toward the caves of prehistoric man?

Sleep rejects me.
I pace back years
to those victims
the Gestapo condemned as guilty.
I pace forward to the years
they were found innocent
in the cemetery.
Look, they rise up,
stand like trees
and look for their executioners.
What a joke.
The world is full of sins.
But sinners?
Not a one.
Crimes have no criminals
today.
Sleep rejects me.
I pace. I reach for paper.
But does anyone read or hear?
Are you listening, anyone?
My love?
My friend?
My brother?
My awesome century?
Give me sleep
or wake up every man
who sleeps this lie.
Sleep rejects me.

[20]

CLEVER LAMB

"The clever lamb sucks on two mothers."

Why bother
maneuvering
back and forth
between two?

It will only
hasten
your journey
into lamb stew.

Gentlemen:
you torture yourselves
in vain.

You are losing sleep
trying to unlock
the secret of
cancer.

Do you want to find
the key
to life itself?

It is so simple.
So ordinary.

Man is a hard mass
and unforgiving . . .
Surrounded by thieves
who want to steal his life,

he persists in
carrying around
a childish grudge.

Then suddenly
a sister
(or brother,
or best friend)
lands in the
hospital

and everything
changes

but only
when he learns
from a whisper
from the shadows
over the bed

that visiting hours
are over.

FIREFLY

Stupid insect,
oh why
did you show off
your dazzling position
and die?
Your enemies snuffed
out that spark
and left us
in the doubled dark.

PASSING A PREGNANT WOMAN

Whoever you are
you have become a god now.
No, the mother of God.
Even if you had been the despised
whore, you have become clean now,
just as soil and manure become holy,
and no longer soil nor manure
when flowers bloom through.

Whenever I pass you,
I am filled with awe
at your inward eye

and ear that hears
what we cannot hear,
your smile for the smiling one within,
tears with the tearful one within.

Like the seven dolls
in the Russian toy,
you carry within you a child,
the child carries the child
she will bear and that child, the child
that she will bear and . . .
I love your tears that come for no reason.

I love the benevolence
of gods with two hearts.

In the orchard at twilight
as the trees fall asleep
I'm picking cherries
from the smallest of trees.

In the dusk the tree trembles
as if it is being disrobed,

and I feel as it shivers
as if I'm slipping off
the jewels from the ears
of my little love.

Perhaps they are not even guilty, God,
this unsinging pack, my enemies.
If you made me a nightingale, why throw
me into a flock of crows like these?

And if you bleached me pale and white,
why toss me in the black brood
where every dark beak could peck,
attracted to the white mark, to draw blood?

And why was I, the object of attack
and puncture, also dropped into the pit
to be struck by vipers and snakes
again, wise God? Perhaps was it

because birds evolved from reptiles
and every crawling thing
cannot forgive the flight of birds
so great its envy of their wings?

It may be this swarm that cannot sing
is guilty of no crime at all
but having a nightingale flung to it.
God, why did you make me fall?

I had a dark and paralyzing
dream of strangulation. And
now I am told it was not
a nightmare but quite true.
A strangler caught my throat
and with one hand choked me
while his other clamped
my mouth and nose. Then
at the last moment of my
struggle with death
I found breath enough to
gasp a last rasping Help!
And the strangler turned
to others to sneer, "Listen
to that. He calls himself
a poet. Listen to that
voice, that tone. Where
is its gentle music and
sense of harmony? Poet,
indeed. I call that nerve."

Lake and plains do not make a homeland,
nor common language, nor shared hymn.
I withdraw my claim to call you mother
while you are mistress to oppression, Spain.

I refuse to render to Caesar
coinage minted for heaven by God.
Let me choose eternal oblivion
to pragmatic poetry's gold crown.

I reject the bribery of prizes.
The reward of Teuton treachery is shame.
I repudiate silence before power.
I play Don Quixote, if you are Franco.

I relinquish the rites of debate
when your argument is based on spite.
I reject prowling in packs;
I was not born a wolf but man.

I refuse to talk or write a language
that has crushed truth out of words.
I repudiate even listening. To hear
is to be accomplice to its crimes.

I give up my struggle against you.
My one weapon has been stained.
I even forswear inhaling.
You have poisoned the air we breathe in.

I renounce this generation, this era,
that cannot distinguish wet from dry,
and give up my one and only life
condemned to be spent in this time.

O tyrants, how gratified you must be
to reduce the poet's flame to ash.
But I myself put the full stop to my sentence
before you auction off honor and my name.

I know that all the saints are old hat
and discarded and
all the new temples outdated
before their paint is dry.
Nowadays
the only novelty is vice.
Bell and book are old fashioned.
Only life throbs: New! New!
even as it ebbs away.

Let man's mind snare the sun,
his chest still bellows
with a Neanderthal heart!

O poet,
your part in this crazy century is
crazy lover.
You are not the husband
nor the butler in this play.

But you know that even tomorrow's
Le Monde is outdated. The only news
is in the "Songs of Songs."

No, not yet, trees.
This is a false start. A fake.
After the endless freeze,
this thaw is a trap. Wait.

It is an ambush.
Don't bud. Winter is back
to trick you, acting like spring.
Keep track

before you turn to ice,
tighten each bud
like a fist and fight.
Stand fast.

Stand up to this false start
in the name of the true spring
to come at last.

ART

It is hard to tell
the truth from sham,
gold from gloss,
gem from glass.

We give the genuine
away that would
adorn us best
and keep the paste.

Not everyone's a man.
Like the jeweler's trade
humanity is learned.
A man is not born. He's made.

What are we anyway,
we the people
of this land?
What are we?
If the conversation
gets too frank,
we avert
our eyes.
If we were a ship,
we would be
aground.
If we were a clay
vessel, we would be
full of tears.
If we were soil,
we would have turned
to stone with horror.
If we were stone,
we would have
cracked with pain.

We are a great soul
with no flesh;
a rare talent
with no tools,
a brave general
with no army,
a worshipper
of a past
which lies in ruin.

What are we
anyway,
we and our land?

If the talk
gets explicit,
we turn our eyes.

We are tourists
in our own country,
guests
in our own home,
a land without
inhabitants,
a people without
land,
scattered pearls
lost beyond
the collecting.

What more can you do
to him who is already
flat on the ground?

If he were on a throne,
on top of a heap of praise,
a pile of profit or
the peak of fame,

you might undermine,
topple or push him down.

But he is already in the dirt. Where
will you shove him to?
What more can you do?

I am an Armenian, ancient as this Biblical Ararat,
my feet still wet from the waters of the flood.
Mine, the sacred land that Noah first beheld;
mine, the sword that cut down the Babylonian Pel.

The moss that grows on these old stones is not so old
as my blood that cemented them in altars for the first
sun in Khaldean temples, long before
either Massis or I had learned to sigh,

long before flowers and cypress forests were dyed
in the blood of my martyred kin; before every hill
became a tomb for brave men and
before every stone a fragment of a stele.

I am an Armenian, ancient as this mountain.
A thousand swords have clashed against my shield
and every sword and scabbard fallen back
were crushed while like my mountain I stayed upright.

Every century has cut a frown into my soul,
scattered my children over the skin of the world,
uprooted tree and reed and left the lowly bush,
plunged Ararat into new tides of blood.

But like Noah, saved from the deluge to walk
down from Ararat to towns of silent stone,
I live again with the stubborn orphan's will
and light my lamp with my own blood as oil.

[37]

And having gathered my wandering children,
found them through tears, rebuilt their nest,
unrusted ploughs, I will find new Nareks to sing
redemption for the holocaust.

I am an Armenian old as this Ararat.
No mountain could have stood
as many blows from every Attila
from every marauding horde.

I endured. Hardened myself for centuries
through slaughter, deportation, to stay
like the eternal snow on the twin peaks
preserving a handful of wheat to re-sow.

How shall I praise this miracle?
There are so few syllables of joy
which Mesrob's alphabet can form, —
since the first Attila came.

I am the ancient sprout, the oldest song
of Goghten, mixed with the roar
of bombs. I am an Armenian,
the ancient exile returned

finally to my native house
in this October light
waiting to greet
a Golden Age once more.

FOR AROUS*

There's that smile, elegant
and distant, acknowledging
the audience you captivate.

There caught up in the role
as always, magic actress,
nuances no one else can duplicate.

But this time who cast you
as Queen of Stillness?
Although you are center stage,

the part does not suit you
at all. It's lousy,
Arous. Abdicate.

*Actress Arous Voskanian lying in her coffin.

[39]

It used to annoy me to hear
that trite adage of old,
but now I understand and believe
that silence is gold.

It is minted of metal to pay
the man who beholds
the fraud, the murder and plots
for which silence is sold.

Does the sensible man, outraged,
speak? Write? Or shout?
No. It is drilled into all slaves
that silence is gold.

HOME

"The Armenian language is the home of the Armenian."
Moushegh Ishkhan

Torn from our native hearths
we found refuge in our ancient
fortresses and in stone
monasteries until the hand
of the miracle rescued us.
Freed, we made new homes
on foreign soil.

Then deportation again.
This time old fortresses and
monasteries were levelled.
Exiled, with not even the black
rafter nor the dislodged pillar
to rebuild, we were truly
without shelter when, O miracle,
we found "quarters" in the four lines
of old songs and poems.

Everytime an Armenian asks
"Say a house of verse,"
the four lines of the quatrain
become four walls. And the muse fills
its empty treasury with new gold.

We call those jeweled quatrains
"hyrens"
so that even if we forget our letters,

or how to read, the songs
can sing themselves, cut
themselves into stone, and become
a place. Even the song "Homeless"
becomes a home.

Note: *House, Armenian* doun, *means stanza or quatrain.* Hyren
          or quatrain is the most frequently used form of verse in the
          Middle Ages. From doun *is derived* Andouni, *a type of*
          poetry or song of exile.

[42]

You never existed.
You were a legend,
a tale for telling
and for books.
If you were a state, a country,
the king's palace was a prison,
his crown the fist of a stranger,
his throne the witness box
of the accused.
Your rule was reignless,
your home, exile,
your state, statement,
your republic, silence,
your seal the hoofprint
of the Mongol horse.
Was your totem the wolf?
The eagle? The bear?
No.
Merely a wise but too kind man
drained pale for centuries,
exhausted from denying evil,
singing goodness,
wearied from his own
faith.

You never existed.
You were a legend,
a tale, a myth.

Listen to this strange tale.
I did everything
I could for this apple
(the only apple)
to ripen and redden
so that it would be
my cryptogram,
my poem, my gift
to this world, to my century.

And yes, it reddened
beautifully and
I picked it,
sliced it, then
froze with anguish.

A black worm wriggled
in my one
and only
apple. It was as if
that red skin were a blush
of shame. Do you understand
my story?
I did not have another apple.
I had not planted another tree.

I love your stony roads,
your ancient songs,
your poplar trees

and swallows above the fields
that loop like eagles
swooping down.
I love those fragrant fields
promising recurrent springs . . .

I love the village people
early in the morning,
reaping
in sight of mountains that I love.

I love the jagged mountains
fragmented like old monuments . . .
I love the night they rest against.

And though I cannot deny,
I love life
and its daily living.

Should anyone take what is left of you
I will embrace death gladly
in the name of life, Armenia.

I finally found
(although too late for me)
the door to happiness
has a simple, old key.

Feel seven times
before you strike or speak.
If you write in fury
don't mail for a week.

Everyone need not like you.
Find your own voice.
Choosing is easy but joyless
when you have no choice.

Love if you can
for your heart to survive.
But if you can't love easily,
love is exercise.

Act as one man
although you know nine parts.
Greet the tragic as comic;
life imitates art.

You are the dream
to mend my heart,
but insomnia
keeps us apart.

Poor thing. Poor crippled measure
of punctuation. Who would know,
who could imagine you used to be
an exclamation point?
What force bent you over?
Age, time and the vices
of this century?
Did you not once evoke,
call out and stress?
But you got weary of it all,
got wise, and turned like this.

GOSSIP

"The barking dog does not stop the caravan."

If you should read tomorrow
in some poison pen
Gazette
that you have stolen
a star from heaven
(and there's even
a witness
to your theft),
do not bother to deny it,
nor defend yourself. Lies
thrive on gossip.
And each denial gathers aura
to the lie.

Somehow accept
a small degree
of guilt. For instance,

if you were reported
seen in Paris
on Brigitte Bardot's knee,
say: Oh, how you wish
that it were true.

Or if accused
of robbing Chase Manhattan,
laugh, saying you wish
that too could be.

In this world each does
what he needs to do.
Dogs must bark,
but the caravan proceeds.

[49]

Say "Good Morning" to the aged brightly.
They stay half in darkness even
while they answer you politely
grateful to have escaped the night again.

Ask about their sleep. But not gruffly.
They've spent half the night in fighting
death. Don't fight them. Let them
thank God for the victory of light.

Say "Good Morning" to the aged lightly.
Don't load burdens on their shoulders.
It's bad enough just being older.
Time is heavy enough.

I love your hands
which hold me,
held me,
for so many years
without
binding me,

hands which make
me master
without mastering me,

encircle
without
strangling me,

lift me
the way the drowning
man is lifted,

hands
whose cupped shells
change me
slowly slowly
into the pearl
they wanted
all the time.

The music is hot and low,
and a beautiful woman
is undulating with its rhythms.
"S'il vous plait, madame,
what is your name?''

Is she dancing,
singing,
about to do
a comedy routine?
No.
She is removing her clothes
one by one.

Oh, the eternal masculine wish
is about to be granted here.
A miracle.
Under the flashing lights
the flash of white flesh—
thighs revealed,
and she moves hips and breasts,
each white
with an eye of fire.

Now even the fig leaf
will fall in the uninhibited
Eden as Madame Eve
sways and shivers.

Oh yes, the male's eternal
wish, granted.
And you, waiting for this moment,
why are you not burning up?

Why are you sitting there
so coolly
when at this very moment,
if your wish had not been
granted,
you would have given anything
just to undo one button
of the same girl's blouse?

CLIMB

I had been climbing steadily
and paused
when voices from below rejoiced,
''Aha, at last, he stops.''

They're wrong, of course, I will go on
because
only the falling rock stays
at rest where it drops.

QUESTION

Your child turns
to you with ''why's.''
You answer or
you improvise.

You turn to God
with your concerns
and wonder to whom
He turns.

NIGHT

Heavy
black
dreams
hang
on the thin
string of my
sleep
like
over-sized
prayer beads . . .
and who
knows
what
they mean.

CLOCK

Yesterday
life stretched quite limitless.
I had time to travel,
but the roads were blocked ahead.

Now today
all roads are open wide
and beckon me to go.
It's time that is fled.

When I am tired and tortured
by time and the harsh land,
when tears and songs
do not appease or ease,
I come here to sit
upon this stone
in the shadow of stones
as in the past.
I look down the path of dust
to the orchards
swimming in a mist ahead.
Orchards of Ashtarag below
the sky pierced by St. Mary's dome . . .
I come to the tombstones
of my ancestors beside
the River Kassakh that cuts
through the earth and goes
like the lives of men,
like mine. We are transients
in this air, who love this
earth so much. We stay
to rest our heads forever
upon it here.

SEA

The man on the shore shouts
"What are you, sea?"
The ocean echoes,
"You see.

"You see surf and sand
where you dump trash.
You think you rule these waves.
You forget you pass.

"Man's tiny lies and passions
drown in my roar and
fall as sand does
through the fingers of his hand."

The man shouts "Fine.
But some of us have won
and stopped you with a line.
Byron. Ayvasovsky.* Hugo."

The ocean echoes, "You go."

*Famous Armenian painter of sea scenes.

[59]

AT THE AIRPORT IN EREVAN
(waiting for William Saroyan's ashes)

In this very place, yesterday,
we waited for you to come down
from the plane. We waited for your words, songs, jokes,
warm shadow, a mountain's, on the road. Like Andok's shadow,
like Tsovassar's.
What is this?
What kind of homecoming?
Ashes and tears.
How can I say welcome to
an American vase?
Parev. Parov. No.
Let who can speak
speak. Something is wrong
when such a voice is still.
Speak. How can you be still
with your thousand graces,
million words, you
who loved to sing
the song of earth,
so still, dear crazy Bitlistzi?

SONG FOR THE CRANE

Where do you come from , crane?
I ache to hear your call,
to know you come from home.
Have you any news at all?
                    Koutchag

There were ashes on your wings
when you were in Armenia last;
your eyes welled with tears
too deep, too vast to tell.

You flew off from your nest
abandoned like the land,
vowing never to return
where pillage and death reign.

Wherever you went, dear crane,
you never escaped the past.
In every foreign land
Armenians called your name.

Wherever you went, crane,
you found a prison and new pain
without a place of rest;
ashes in each nest.

However blue the sky
their questions followed you,
the exiles' need for news
and you with no reply.

[61]

Since death was everywhere,
you turned to die at home,
passed Ararat once more
where new roses grow from stone.

Come back, dear crane, come home
and bury the exiles' grief
to where Massis bends now
in envy to the east.

A thousand welcomes, crane.
Let us heal your broken heart.
Bring all the wanderers want.
Bring all the exiles need.

AVE MARINA

(To Marina Tsvetayeva)

Your heartbreak was wider
than the size of your heart.

Blacker than the night
your inner dark.

Larger than your eyes
the tears that fell.

With more depth than your mind,
the profundities that welled.

Your fate was more devious
than your means of escape.

Deeper than flesh
your bruise and pain.

Louder than your lyre
the song it played.

And your debt to torture
more than a lifetime could pay.

[63]

AFTERWORD

Illuminating the Heart of Armenia

On a summer evening in 1962 I was sitting on the balcony of Gevorg Emin's apartment, with him and Barouyr Sevag, the other major modern Armenian poet. While we talked the city of Erevan floated before us in a peaceful sea of lights. The lights reminded Barouyr Sevag of Emin's background in electrical engineering. Emin was pleased, even proud, that his first and only hydro-electric plant in Vartenis was still in operation, even after the construction of atomic power plants. It was still operating, illuminating the heartland of Armenia.

In recalling that evening I am struck by the fact that Emin's poetry is doing the very same thing as the hydro-electric plant, illuminating Armenia's heart.

He and Barouyr Sevag were the first of the generation of Armenian poets who followed the bold and innovative Eghishe Charents to free Armenian poetry from the restrictions that followed Charents's time, the bleak Stalin era.

The restraints of the time that bound up the literature following Charents were both political and stylistic. A formalism had returned. And, ironically, the poetry of Avedik Issahakian and Hovaness Toumanian was in favor, although these two poets were in no way connected to, nor expressed the revolutionary fervor of the new regime. The experimentalism of Charents was discarded; vision and originality discouraged for several decades.

The distinguished literary historian Manoug Abeghian was pressed into service to reform spelling and standardize the language. Rigid new rules and spelling made root recognition and coinage of new vocabulary almost impossible. Language and poetry suffered until Emin and Sevag with their classical training, and in Emin's case, scientific expertise, plus their own insights, made Armenian poetry new and explosive again.

Emin's poetry was free of the oriental haziness that had gradually crept into the tradition after medieval times. Classical Armenian poetry had been characterized by lyricism, brevity and intensity. Emin's

[65]

poetry often recalls those crisp *hyrens* (quatrains) of the medieval bards. His craft, his uniquely powerful style is characterized by an economy of words. He has, too, a Brechtian, enigmatic twist to his loyalty to Soviet internationalism. He avoids the flatness of social-realism, as well as oriental excesses. He is not parochial. In his poem addressing Lorca's executioners he includes *all* executioners.

His poetry develops in three concentric circles beginning with the nucleus of the personal. The second circle, composed of more complex work, deals with the collective sentiments rising from Armenian history and tragedies. In this body of work the Mt. Ararat symbol of the eternity of the Armenian people is a favorite metaphor. In spite of the sadness of the experiences of his people, Emin's outlook remains robust and optimistic.

French poet Louis Aragon has said of Emin's stoic treatment of the tragedies: "What distinguishes Gevorg Emin's work from his predecessors is not so much his elimination of lament and dirge from his writing but his innovative approach to his subject. His is a deliberate attempt to preserve. His unique approach to life is revealed throughout his entire poetry. It is indeed surprising that this refreshing voice is heard from Armenia, which at one time was portrayed as the valley of tears."

The outermost circle of Emin's poetry touches man in his universal aspirations and sadness. His subject is man himself: "*Is there anything else/ more powerful/ or more fragile/ than this thing/ reaching the moon/ chaining the atom/ but always the same transparent clay?*"

He sees the specific tragedies of the Armenians and Jews within the context of universal human tragedy:

> Twentieth Century,
> your thinking machines drink
> blood from Der Zor and Auschwitz.

Emin's ingenious use of puns and emotional tensions, his wit plus his innate aversion to sentimentality, often make his work seem deceptively simple. Yet he is acknowledged as one of the most original and interesting of poets, not only in Armenia but in all the Soviet republics. Barouyr Sevag, who died in 1972, had said even then, "Emin is counted among the top ten most important poets in the Soviet Union. He has developed a full-blooded and powerful poetry which is at times a witness, a prosecutor, and attorney for a trial which is called the Twentieth Century. He has the feel for modern times and knows how to elevate the personal to the universal, how to develop the phenomenal from a single fact. Emin has never sung the song of the pseudo-populist, the belated troubadour, the soured conservative because he is a man belonging to the modern era. Here is a man who knows too much, but never talks too much. He does not develop a subject, he intensifies, he concentrates it. He is more interested in the tree's trunk than its branches and leaves. That is why his message is so sobering."

Emin's tremendous popularity is not confined to the Soviet Union. His books have been translated into more than a dozen languages, including Bulgarian, Latvian, Polish, Russian, Azerbaijani, Arabic, and English. Although this is his first volume in the United States, English volumes were issued in Moscow of a volume of poetry and his prize-winning prose epic "Seven Songs About Armenia," which was also made into a film. Emin is prolific. He has thirty volumes of poetry, including five revised editions.

Individual translations of his poems done by American poet Diana Der Hovanessian have been appearing in American publications since 1972. This book integrates their two talents into one poetic thrust. Together here they seem to speak in one voice which reverberates in many directions and dimensions. Emin's images, like his one and only hydraulic plant, illuminate the heartland of Armenia and move beyond those borders, bringing the light of Ashtarag to the new world.

Edmond Y. Azadian

Gevorg Emin lives in his native Armenia in the Soviet Union. His poetry has been translated into Russian by Pasternak and into almost every other modern language. He was trained in the sciences and was graduated from the Polytechnic Institute, Yerevan, Armenia in the same year as his first book of poetry was published. The author of numerous books, he won the top Soviet literature prizes in literature in 1979 and 1984.

Diana Der Hovanessian, an award-winning American poet whom Saroyan called "a rare and enormous talent," is the translator and co-editor of *Anthology of Armenian Poetry*; *Sacred Wrath, The Selected Poems of Vahan Tekeyan*; *The Arc, Selected Poems of Shen-Mah*; and the forthcoming *Land of Fire, Poems of Eghishe Charents*—all with the scholar Marzbed Margossian. Her own poems have appeared in leading literary publications, including *American Scholar, Harper's, American Poetry Review,* and *The Nation,* and are collected in *How to Choose Your Past*. She is a visiting poet in the Massachusetts schools, and has worked as visiting faculty and writer-in-residence at various universities.